JOURNEYING WITH JESUS

JOURNEYING WITH JESUS

PERSONAL REFLECTIONS ON THE STATIONS OF THE CROSS AND RESURRECTION

EDITED BY
LUCY RUSSELL

ILLUSTRATIONS BY JAMES EDGAR

B L O O M S B U R Y
LONDON • NEW DELHI • NEW YORK • SYDNEY

A Continuum book

Bloomsbury Publishing Plc
50 Bedford Square
London WC1B 3DP

www.bloomsbury.com

Bloomsbury Publishing, London, New Delhi, New York and Sydney

A CIP record for this book is available from the British Library.

ISBN 9781408182079
10 9 8 7 6 5 4 3 2 1

Typeset by Fakenham Prepress Solutions, Fakenham, Norfolk
NR21 8NN

Printed and bound by CPI Group (UK) Ltd, Croydon, CRO 4YY

For my family and Father Duncan Lourensz, with love and thanks.

CONTENTS

The Stations of the Resurrection

PREFACE

Every year my Parish Priest invites parishioners to write their own meditations on the Stations of the Cross. A visitor who came along on one Good Friday for the public devotion was afraid she'd missed the promised coffee and hot cross buns after the service: 'I've been sitting in the Church re-reading the Stations. They really spoke to me. Your Parish Stations seemed so relevant to my own life'. Christ's journey is our journey. The Stations of the Cross – and Resurrection – are about us now, as much as they are about Jesus then.

The Stations of the Cross, also known as the Via Crucis (the Way of the Cross) or the Via Dolorosa (the Way of Sorrows), developed from an early tradition in the Holy Land to follow the Way of the Cross, stopping and contemplating the events of Christ's Passion at the places where tradition held they took place. Some trace the history of these devotions to Mary the mother of Jesus, who may have visited the locations of the Passion and Resurrection after Christ's ascension. Because not everyone could make a pilgrimage to the Holy Land, during the Middle Ages the practice of erecting the Stations in local churches developed as a way of bringing Jerusalem to the people. Throughout history the number and names of the Stations have changed, but the following 14 have become traditional:

Jesus is condemned to death;
Jesus takes up his cross;
Jesus falls the first time;
Jesus meets his mother;
Simon of Cyrene carries the cross;
Veronica wipes the face of Jesus;
Jesus falls the second time;
Jesus meets the daughters of Jerusalem;
Jesus falls the third time;
Jesus is stripped of his garments;
Jesus is nailed to the cross;
Jesus is crucified;
Jesus is taken down from the cross;
Jesus' body is laid in the tomb.

Not all of the events which make up the traditional stations are described in the Gospels; the Third, Fourth, Sixth, Seventh, and Ninth Stations are missing from these accounts, as is St Alphonsus' description of Jesus' body being laid in the arms of his mother in the Thirteenth Station; there is no reference to the *Pieta* in the Gospel accounts.

On Good Friday at the Colosseum in Rome, Pope John Paul II and Pope Benedict XVI have in some years meditated on a Scriptural Way of the Cross, which Pope John Paul II introduced in 1991. This follows the Gospel accounts of Jesus' Passion and death more closely:

Jesus in the garden of Gethsemane;
Jesus is betrayed by Judas and arrested;
Jesus is condemned by the Sanhedrin;
Jesus is denied by Peter;
Jesus is judged by Pilate;
Jesus is scourged and crowned with thorns;
Jesus takes up his cross;
Simon helps Jesus carry his cross;
Jesus meets the daughters of Jerusalem;
Jesus is crucified;
Jesus promises a place in his kingdom to the good thief;
Jesus entrusts Mary and John to each other;
Jesus dies on the cross;
Jesus is laid in the tomb.

The Resurrection

The problem with ending with the Fourteenth Station of the Cross is that it ignores the most important part of our faith: the Resurrection. More recently liturgists have argued that the story of Christ's Passion is incomplete without the Resurrection as the Fifteenth Station. Christ's passion only makes sense when seen in context; after all, the Paschal mystery is twofold. St Alphonsus talks about the Resurrection in his meditation on the Fourteenth Station:

> Oh, my buried Jesus, I kiss the stone that closes You in. But You gloriously did rise again on the third day. I beg You by Your resurrection that I may be raised gloriously on the last day…

The inclusion of the Fifteenth Station is relatively new. In 1979 a representation of an empty tomb was added to the original Stations on the hillside at Lourdes, which were constructed between 1898 and 1911.

The crucifixion is not an end in itself. For early Christians the emphasis would not have been on the cross, but on the empty tomb. We understand the pain and misery; it is harder for us to accept the glory and redemption. And yet, this is the whole point of Christ's Passion. Christ's journey does not end at the cross on Good Friday. His journey continues. He rises from the dead; appears to his friends; ascends to heaven; and with his Father sends the Spirit. His journey says to us, 'I suffered too. Suffering is part of life. But take comfort, have faith. Death is not the end. I am risen and in heaven, and one day you can be too. There will be freedom, peace and justice'. We continue our journey of faith beyond the cross, comforted – as Margaret Mizen reflects in her powerful meditation on the Thirteenth Station – by the Easter promise.

'And suddenly there was a great earthquake; for an angel of the Lord, descending from heaven, came and rolled back the stone and sat on it.' (Matthew 28.2). The stone is not rolled away so that Christ can walk out of the tomb. The stone is rolled away to show that Christ is not there. But as Professor Russell Stannard emphasises, this emptiness is not synonymous with nothingness or absence; Christ died, reflects Sister Wendy Beckett, but he is not dead. At first Mary Magdalen believes Christ's body has been taken somewhere, but this is not a story about body snatching – though St Matthew tells us this is what the religious authorities at the time would have liked everyone to believe:

> After the priests had assembled with the elders, they devised a plan to give a large sum of money to the soldiers, telling them, 'You must say, "His disciples came by night and stole him away while we were asleep."' (Matthew 28.12-14)

For Mary Magdalen it takes a leap of faith to begin to accept what has really happened to Jesus; to stop clinging to the past, and turn to embrace a new reality and believe.

Even the addition of the Fifteenth Station fails to bring into balance the suffering of Christ with his Resurrection, which is why in the 1990s Father Sabino Palumbieri, a Salesian Priest, wrote the Stations of the Resurrection (or Via Lucis; The Way of Light). He wanted to focus on the hope and promise of Christianity which, while intrinsic in the Stations of the Cross, is obscured by the emphasis on suffering. The Stations of the Resurrection emphasise the central event of Christianity: the hope, joy, and promise of the Resurrection. The Way of Light also has 14 stations:

Jesus rises from the dead;
Peter and John arrive at the empty tomb;
The risen Lord appears to Mary Magdalen;
Jesus appears to two disciples on the road to
     Emmaus;
The risen Lord is recognised in the breaking
     of bread;
Jesus appears to his disciples in a locked
     room;

Jesus gives the power to forgive sins;
The risen Lord confirms the faith of Thomas;
The risen Lord meets his disciples on the
    shore of Galilee;
The risen Lord appoints Peter the Head of
    the Church;
The risen Lord sends his disciples to
    evangelise all nations;
The risen Lord ascends to the Father;
Mary and the apostles pray for the coming of
    the Holy Spirit;
Jesus sends the promised Holy Spirit on Mary
    and the apostles.

This new devotion was blessed in Turin on Easter Sunday in 1994 at the Hill of Becchi, the birthplace of St John Bosco, who founded the Society of St Francis de Sales. Fourteen wood carvings by Giovanni Dragoni were displayed on the Hill. Today, they can be seen at Colle Don Bosco. Another set of these Stations by Giovanni Dragoni, in metal, is displayed outdoors at the San Callisto Catacombs.

Personal meditations
In 1985 Pope John Paul II began asking people to compose meditations for his Good Friday prayer service rather than using traditional texts. Pope

Benedict XVI has continued this practice. Over the years, bishops and theologians, priests and religious women, an international group of journalists, and a married couple have all been invited to write meditations. The Stations of the Cross and Resurrection are about more than remembering historical events. Jesus represents us, and when we pray the Stations we are making our own journey too. Christ's Passion and Resurrection give us the courage to face our own suffering: Jesus, his mother, and those that met him on his way of the cross and after he has risen from the dead, all have lessons to teach us relevant to our own lives. There is much to be said for the idea of personalising the Stations and making our devotion relevant to our own journey of faith, and our prayer relevant to current concerns.

My own spiritual understanding of the Stations has developed since I had my children. We have come to think it was a woman called Veronica who reached out and wiped Jesus' face. In fact, we don't know what this woman was called; 'Veronica' is Latin in origin and means 'true image'. But when I think of 'Veronica' wiping the face of Jesus, I remember my midwife reaching towards me and wiping my face when I was in labour. She could do nothing to make my pain stop, but her caring act was welcome. My elder son was a late February baby. In the early days and weeks after his arrival my Mass attendance was non-existent as I strived to get back on my feet and into some sort of family routine. The first time I went to church after James was born was for the Stations of the Cross during Holy Week. James was six weeks old. Never before had I been so struck by Mary's plight. I didn't want to imagine being in her place; but as our then Parish Priest read the Fourth Station, Jesus meets his mother, from Cardinal Newman's Stations of the Cross, I couldn't help it. As I listened, I thought of James asleep in his cot at home, safe and warm. How could I protect him and keep him safe as he grew? As Margaret Mizen's meditation on the Thirteenth Station illustrates so poignantly, there comes a point when I can't guarantee the children's safety. We all face our own heartbreaks. What must Mary have felt as she witnessed the crucifixion?

Why did God let it happen?
In her meditation Ann Widdecombe reflects on the disappointment and sadness of Jesus' closest family and friends: he was God, why didn't he come down from the cross and walk away with them? *Why was he letting this happen?* It is a question we ask when we hear a particularly sad or harrowing news story, or experience a tragedy ourselves. Although we trust

that there is a divine plan this isn't always easy to accept. In the Garden of Gethsemane Christ questions God: does this really have to happen? Isn't there another way? On the cross Christ shows anger, he cries out, 'My God, my God, why have you forsaken me?' (Mark 15.34; Matthew 27.46). This moment reveals a funda-, mental paradox: the presence of God when he seems most absent. The feeling of emptiness can sometimes be so great that only God can fill it. St John of the Cross talked about the idea of the dark night of the soul, and the notion that the darker it is and the more alone you feel, the closer you may be to God. Suffering is part of life and God is present in the darkness, but it doesn't follow that suffering is a good thing. In his reflection on the Twelfth Station, Robin Baird-Smith questions the strand of Christian thinking which says suffering should be accepted passively and is good for the soul. In 1994 Robin's wife and middle child were killed in a road accident. He didn't feel the comfort from God that Margaret Mizen describes as she lay on her bed on the night of her son's death. He felt angry with God. It is an anger he has learned to live with and has described as God's creative activity within him. In his meditation he discusses the issue of Christ's anger on the cross, and suggests God doesn't expect us to be submissive, but to be challenged and to answer back.

When she was falsely arrested, tried and convicted of handling the explosives used by the IRA in the 1974 Guildford bombing, Anne Maguire couldn't believe what was happening. She fought with God. She was innocent. Why would no-one believe her? *Why was God letting this happen?* The question is repeated, over and over again, in response to personal tragedies and national disasters. In his Thought for the Day for Radio 4's *Today* programme on 30 July 2011, the Reverend Dr Joel Edwards considered whether it can really be said that God stands idly by as human disasters unfold. As the drought and famine in the Horn of Africa hit the headlines, he reflected:

> And, where is God in all of this? Always an awkward question for people of faith and a veiled trump card for non-belief. But even as we watch the unfolding events it's not difficult to imagine that any god worth the name may also be asking: where were we?

Joel emphasises the need for the human response to meet the divine response, and it is this theme of the human meeting the divine that he draws upon in his meditation on the Fourth Station. Here he talks about the difficulty our lack of understanding presents, and suggests that it is when we are at our most confounded that we find hope, and God.

Anne Maguire was imprisoned along with her husband, two of her sons, her brother-in-law, and two family friends. Collectively known as the Maguire Seven, their convictions were quashed in June 1991, after they had served their full sentences. Anne's faith grew and sustained her throughout her nine years in prison. Like Jesus himself, Anne was arrested on false charges and became a prisoner. We are so used to the story of the Passion and Resurrection that sometimes we forget that Jesus ends his life on earth as a convicted criminal; executed alongside other criminals (Luke 23.39-44). Anne's experience leads me to reflect on Danny McAllister's Station, Simon of Cyrene carries the cross: we are never in a position to judge, and it isn't usually convenient or part of our plan to stop what we are doing to help, but *anyone* can find themselves a prisoner.

In his reflection on the Ninth Station, Rabbi Dr Jonathan Romain contemplates the relationship and similarities between Judaism and Christianity. The links between the Abrahamic faiths are strong. Discussion about Judaism and the existence of God inevitably leads to questions about God's presence or absence during events like the Holocaust; to borrow words from Joel Edwards, 'a trump card for non-belief'. It is an especially difficult question, but I find Rabbi Hugo Gryn's understanding of this moving and revelatory, 'God was there [in Auschwitz] himself, violated and blasphemed.' Hugo tells how as a 14 year old in the Liberose concentration camp on Yom Kippur, the Day of Atonement, he fasted and hid amongst the stacks of insulation boards. He tried to remember the prayers that he had learned as a child at synagogue and asked God for forgiveness. Eventually, he said, 'I dissolved in crying. I must have sobbed for hours... Then, I seemed to be granted a curious inner peace... I believe God was also crying... I found God.' But it was not the God of his childhood, the God who was expected to miraculously rescue the Jewish People.

Throughout the New Testament our relationship with God develops from the model of a 'father' and his children, or a 'master' and his servants. In her meditation Ruth Burrows calls Christ our brother, and notes that he invites us to be his friends (John 15.15). There is an equality here, and we have to assume some responsibility. In his letter to the Hebrews St Paul explains that we are expected to grow up and develop spiritually (Hebrews 5.12-13). We are expected to have an opinion and for this to inform our action. As Chris Bain reflects it is we, not God, who condemn eight million children a year to die from preventable disease. Una Kroll and Antony Feltham-White reflect on the effects of war. It is we, not God, who are responsible for the wars which see such suffering. 'What would Jesus say?' asked anti-Capitalist protestors when Occupy set up camp outside St Paul's Cathedral in London in October 2011. It is a valid question. During his historic visit to the UK in 2010, Pope Benedict XVI highlighted Blessed John Henry Newman's teaching that there can be no separation between what we believe and the way we live our lives. While he was in the UK, the Pope congratulated Baroness Warsi – the first Muslim woman to be a Cabinet member – on her defence of faith and asked her to continue to make the case for faith to have a role in society. The Abrahamic faiths not only share similar histories (all tracing their origins to Abraham) and common core values, but together they represent the voice of faith in an aggressively secular age. On the morning of the Resurrection, Mary Magdalen initially experienced difficulty in believing who Christ was. In modern society we can experience difficulty in professing our belief in Christ. How far are we prepared to stand up and be counted? This is a question Peter Hitchens raises in his reflection.

Robin Baird-Smith quotes from Job 38.3; God responds to Job's lament, 'Brace yourself like a fighter; I am going to ask the questions, and you are to inform me!' God is interested in our lives. He has given us the freedom to make our own choices, but he is intimately concerned with what path we choose and our response to what lies along that path; he is ready to walk with us on our journey, and to listen to what we have to say. I would like to thank all those who have shared what they have to say in these Stations.

The Stations of the Cross

Jesus is condemned to death

Chris Bain

The condemnation by the Sanhedrin seems a formality. On the face of it, Jesus' answers to the priests, to Herod, and to Pilate were cool and measured. But we know that, aware of his fate, the human Jesus had spent an agonising vigil the previous night at Gethsemane, sweating blood. He had suffered beatings and humiliation. Most damningly, he was betrayed by those he loved, and who said they loved him.

The thing is, it was love in the dock: the love that was Jesus, forgave sinners, said we must turn the other cheek, wanted the rich to give up their wealth, said we were all equal, spoke familiarly to women, and empowered the poor. He said that what we did to the least of his brothers we did to him; that the most important commandment was love.

This love is uncomfortable, unacceptable, unrealistic, naïve. It is too costly; it breaks all our man-made rules.

More than a billion people today live on less than a pound a day; eight million children a year die before they are five from preventable and treatable disease. The love that is Jesus would be weeping. Pope John Paul II said that we see Christ's face on every poor person in the world; yet still we allow the suffering.

We still condemn him to death.

Jesus, you know what it's like to feel abandoned, betrayed and afraid. Give us the gift of love so we can offer hope and love to those who face death through poverty or war. Amen.

CHRIS BAIN IS DIRECTOR OF CAFOD, THE CATHOLIC OVERSEAS DEVELOPMENT AGENCY.

Jesus takes up his cross

Peter Hitchens

Jesus takes up his cross. But we do not follow his example, if we can avoid it. It is all very well to be reassured that, 'Blessed are ye, when men shall revile you, and persecute you, and shall say all manner of evil against you falsely for my sake.' But in its twenty-first century form, this reviling does not feel blessed. It often just feels embarrassing, which is not especially ennobling. The power of soft persecution is sometimes greater than that of the old-fashioned hard kind. If someone tries to bully us out of our faith, then our pride may compel us to fight for it. But if our enemies more subtly seek to make us look foolish, then we may well give in. We should be readier to understand that, just as Christ is so much greater than we are, our sacrifices and humiliations are bound to seem petty beside his.

But if we allow ourselves to be embarrassed out of our faith, then much worse will follow. And I believe it has done. The Churches have helped this to happen, by themselves being embarrassed by the things they are supposed to say. How many prayers are now about vague and fashionable political causes, which by espousing we do not alter? How many sermons never actually mention God, Christ or the Resurrection? And so we lay down our Cross, and sidle apologetically away, mumbling that we didn't really mean it – and it is just another normal day in Jerusalem.

PETER HITCHENS IS A COLUMNIST FOR *THE MAIL ON SUNDAY*; HE WON THE 2010 ORWELL PRIZE FOR HIS REPORTING OF FOREIGN AFFAIRS. HE IS AUTHOR OF NUMEROUS BOOKS, INCLUDING *THE RAGE AGAINST GOD*.

Jesus falls the first time

Paul Farmer

Most people like to think of themselves as able to cope with the challenges that life throws at them. Most of us find a public exposure of our failings difficult to handle. We get embarrassed when we trip up on a step, or forget our lines in a presentation, or if we slip playing football, allowing the other side to score a goal.

This moment in Jesus' journey, when he falls for the first time, is an immense test of his personal strength and resilience. His physical strength is tested – he's carrying a heavy cross, a cross which will ultimately bear him in his last moments. But it's his mental strength, his resilience, which is being tested the most. He has already been humiliated in public, and is now on this journey, surrounded by a large jeering, hostile crowd. His supporters have evaporated, afraid for their own safety. He is alone, isolated and beaten. His fall is not just one of physical exhaustion, but an expression of mental uncertainty, maybe for the first time.

However, Jesus has profound depths of resilience. He knows what he has to do and is determined to see it through. Whilst down, he perhaps thinks about his conversation with his Father in Gethsemane. His task is simple, to recover, get up and continue on this journey. He does this, doubtless to more jeers, and moves on. His physical strength is sapping, but his mental resolve is as great as ever.

For so many people, the first experiences and signs of a mental health problem are terrifying and incomprehensible. It's unclear what's happening; tasks which previously were simple are now incredibly difficult. You find it difficult to work, sleep or eat properly. You just don't understand what's happening to you, and that's frightening. People around you start treating you differently, because you're behaving differently; 'he's not the person he once was.'

And so the first 'fall' for people is often a frightening moment, but also an important moment of realisation that something isn't as it was. For people with a severe mental health problem, that can involve a hospital admission, but it's more likely to be the moment you go to the GP, that admission of a problem, or maybe tell your boss.

Like Jesus, though, the act of the fall – the moment of admission – is frailty, but it is also a source of strength. You still have some physical and emotional resilience; you can get back up and try again. You need help, but people want to help you. Perhaps now more than ever you are realising who you are and what you have to do to get back up.

Lord, we ask you to give us the resilience to cope with the challenges of life; to recognise our own frailties, and seek your support to overcome them. Help us to be able to learn from our falls, and to be able to recover, stronger from the experience.

PAUL FARMER IS CHIEF EXECUTIVE OF MIND, THE MENTAL HEALTH CHARITY.

Jesus meets his mother

Joel Edwards

She saw him coming up the hill and couldn't believe her eyes. Her Son was bleeding, spat upon with a crown of thorns, carrying a cross. She stood there, the guiltiest woman in Jerusalem. But when their eyes met as he passed, it happened all over again: incomprehensible hope. It was easier to be pregnant with a Saviour than to give birth to an inscrutable Son.

Just for a moment as the crowds closed in behind him, she wasn't sure she had the strength to follow him to the Place of the Skull. Now more than ever, she was still wondering why.

Through all the years, his words of wisdom and turning water into wine, Mary never really understood. But she had always hoped – even now.

It's not just the bad news which defeats us. The mindless killing by a drunk driver, the discovery of a terminal illness, or the fact that our life partner just walked out, are all bad enough. Even the grand scale of injustices in our world which impales the poor and destroys their future is hard to handle. But what really hurts is not knowing why God allows it all and stands back to watch his own reputation pelted by cynicism. It makes it hard to follow him up the hill.

Our worst discomfort is not getting God.

But if Mary has anything redemptive to say to us it's this: hope is probably at its very best in the presence of excruciating uncertainty.

THE REVEREND JOEL EDWARDS IS DIRECTOR OF MICAH CHALLENGE INTERNATIONAL, A GLOBAL CAMPAIGN TO MOBILISE CHRISTIANS AGAINST POVERTY, AND TO INFLUENCE LEADERS OF RICH AND POOR NATIONS TO FULFIL THEIR PROMISE TO ACHIEVE THE MILLENNIUM DEVELOPMENT GOALS. HE IS A REGULAR CONTRIBUTOR TO THOUGHT FOR THE DAY ON BBC RADIO 4.

THE FIFTH STATION

Simon of Cyrene carries the cross

Danny McAllister

It was definitely not the plan.

He had travelled nine hundred miles from Cyrenia, leaving his wife and two sons behind, to be in Jerusalem for the Passover: that was the plan.

His sandal strap had broken and he was on his way to have it mended; nine hundred miles, remember.

If only he had cut through past the baker's, but he had decided to cut across the main drag as it was quicker. He knew there were often 'crims' being brought up to Golgotha to be executed: not his problem.

He was waiting to cross to the cobbler's, aware that a procession to Golgotha was passing by: inconvenient.

He did not know if the prisoners passing were thieves, murderers, rapists or just troublesome but he knew where they were going: not his business.

He saw that one 'crim' was in a right state, kept falling down, staggering – he must have had a right hammering: it happens.

And then, and this he could well do without, he was pulled out of the crowd (why me?) and compelled to help the beat up bloke. Well, actually, the bloke was so done in he ended up carrying the whole cross while the bloke staggered on ahead: hold up.

With the weight lifted the bloke could speak; he spoke to some women, but not to him, at least he didn't think he had; anyway he had his hands full: heavy thing, this.

He was hacked off that by touching the cross he was defiled and would not be able to partake of Passover; what a liberty: nine hundred miles mind.

It's never a convenient time and it's rarely the plan. It is often a right pain and none of our business anyway. Cross carrying is rarely planned in the diary.

Lord, let me carry the cross when it is inconvenient, unplannned, unwelcome, and I could well do without it.

DANNY MCALLISTER CBE IS FORMER DIRECTOR OF HIGH SECURITY IN HER MAJESTY'S PRISON SERVICE.

Veronica wipes the face of Jesus

Ben Bano

I went to see Mum in her residential home last Sunday. She wasn't able to recognise me, and thought I was my Dad. She is not aware that he died a few years ago. I tried so hard to communicate with her and reassure her. I came away from my visit upset that she has deteriorated so quickly – her dementia was only diagnosed three years ago. She spends a lot of time in bed, seemingly oblivious to what is going on around her. I know I need to understand that this is the course of Alzheimer's disease, but it is so difficult to see her in this state.

Today after Mass I had a talk with our priest. He reminded me that, as Mum's mental and physical faculties fail, she needs me and the rest of the family to help her to hold on to her identity. We need to understand that Mum's spiritual self is still intact – and we can nurture it with memories, prayers and hymns which have meant a lot to her during her life.

Mum gets easily upset. But this afternoon I took one of her favourite hymn books to her. We sung together one of the old Welsh hymns she had sung in her childhood. It was lovely to see how her eyes lit up. She gets great pleasure from receiving Communion each Sunday from one of our Eucharistic Ministers.

Lord, I am here before you with Mum at my side. We are in her bedroom – on the walls are pictures of Dad and of special times for both of them. Help me to realise that she is still very precious in your eyes even as her mental and physical faculties fail.

In her weakened state, help me to see her as a gift to you and to us, a source of grace and inspiration to myself and our family.

I have wiped her face before I leave her today. Just as Veronica wiped your face as an act of love in your suffering, I give Mum this act of love – and I pray that she will be ever closer to you as her dementia advances.

BEN BANO IS PRODUCER OF '*IT'S STILL ME, LORD*', A DVD ON UNDERSTANDING AND MEETING THE SPIRITUAL NEEDS OF PEOPLE WITH DEMENTIA, COMMISSIONED BY CARITAS SOCIAL ACTION NETWORK.

Jesus falls the second time

Sheila Hollins

On my knees, beaten, no strength to go on, despite encouragement from those closest to me, I feel despair, it all feels pointless, why did I let myself get so tired? I rage against my aggressors and feel humiliated. If only I had anticipated what they would demand of me. If only I had been better prepared this wouldn't have happened, and my weakness wouldn't have been found out. But then it happens a second time.

And someone shows kindness to me, just a little thing – wiping my brow, offering me some water, helping me to my feet and encouraging me. Hope restores my strength and I struggle on with my load lightened. Thank you whoever you are.

In my reflection on the seventh station, I see in Jesus both the vulnerability and the strength of so many members of our community, and I also see my own struggles. It all depends on how you look at things. As you meditate on this station I ask you too to reflect on any time when you felt vulnerable and on what helped you to overcome those feelings of weakness. Now think about two people you know who you see as dependent on others to protect them from the unkindnesses of life. Perhaps it's the autistic woman worshipping in your parish, who everybody avoids after Mass because of her lack of friends and lack of social skill. Or the person with cerebral palsy who has been mugged more times than he can remember by youths who find it funny that he cannot fight back. But what about the young Mum who takes her seriously disabled child to playgroup and joins the other mothers in helping them to be comfortable with disability rather than staying behind her own closed doors, or the man who gave up his job to care for his wife after she had a stroke and had to face a house move as well when his mortgage became unaffordable.

Jesus allowed himself to become vulnerable to show that he understands the burdens we will encounter in our own lives. His example of falling a second time gives me strength and helps me to believe in the triumph of the cross.

BARONESS SHEILA HOLLINS IS EMERITUS PROFESSOR OF THE PSYCHIATRY OF LEARNING DISABILITY AT ST GEORGE'S, UNIVERSITY OF LONDON, AND A CROSSBENCH LIFE PEER IN THE HOUSE OF LORDS. SHE WAS PRESIDENT OF THE ROYAL COLLEGE OF PSYCHIATRISTS FROM 2005 TO 2008 AND IS PRESIDENT OF THE BRITISH MEDICAL ASSOCIATION.

Jesus meets the daughters of Jerusalem

Una Kroll

'Women of Jerusalem, do not weep for me, but weep for yourselves and for your children too.' (Luke 23.28)

When I was a child, you sent a Jewish refugee and her daughter to our home in England for shelter. I recall their tears, their desperate hope for the father they left behind; hope unfulfilled. I remember the two Polish children who came to live with us during the Second World War. I shared their pain of separation from our roots: for two of my Baltic cousins in the German army died on the Russian front, and the third lingered in a Russian prison for 12 years before eventual release. That is how you taught me compassion for friends and enemies alike. That is how you taught me to cross boundaries that divide us.

That is how you brought me to my work of prayer and reconciliation in conflict situations.

Our tears are our prayers for our own people, yet as we weep we hear the cries of all people throughout your world. We weep with our friends – and with our persecutors too. Such wanton killing, Lord, of the little ones who starve through our greed, those who die of thirst, those who are carelessly killed in war, those who are raped and left to die, those who die as slaves: as you wept, we weep. Your tears, Lord, and your words on the Way to the Cross, inspire in us a desire to help you heal the pain of the world.

So, Lord, help us to find ways to help you to heal the pain of your world. Help us to cross the boundaries that divide us. Help us to treasure your creation so that future generations can live in harmony.

Una Kroll is a former GP and was one of the best-known campaigners for women's ordination. She spent ten years as an Anglican priest before becoming a Catholic in 2008.

Jesus falls for the third time

Jonathan Romain

It happened out of the blue. One moment we were best friends – in fact we had been since we came to the school three years earlier – then suddenly we were fighting each other in the playground during every lunch hour. It was Christians against Jews. I was Jewish, my three friends were Christian, and although that had never been an issue in the past, now we were on opposite sides, while some other eight-year-olds with whom I'd barely spoken before, but who were also Jewish, were fighting alongside me.

I do not know what caused that eruption of religious divisions and, once the headmaster stepped in to reprimand everyone, the lunch time battles ceased and old friendships resumed as if nothing had happened.

We had no idea why being Jewish or Christian mattered so much. Yet, somehow, the prejudices and conflicts of previous generations had re-ignited in us.

Part of me ignored it entirely and carried on with my friendships. Part of me was mortified and it changed my perceptions forever. Up to that point I knew I was Jewish but had not reckoned I was different or a potential target.

The experience could have led me to become insular and mix only with fellow Jews, or to submerge anonymously into gentile company and throw off my Jewish identity. Instead I instinctively felt that being both adamantly Jewish and thoroughly part of wider society might sometimes be painful but was the better path.

It also taught me — though I would not have used such terms at the time — that inter-faith dialogue and improving Jewish-Christian relations was vital. This has to be at ecclesiastical level, with rabbis and priests exploring both our common roots and the reasons for where we diverge. It also has to be at the lay level, encouraging ordinary Christians and Jews to see each other as like themselves.

The stakes are high. It is about social harmony. It is also about rectifying the religious mistakes of the past on both sides. We don't want Jesus to fall a fourth time, or us with him.

RABBI DR JONATHAN ROMAIN MBE IS MINISTER OF MAIDENHEAD SYNAGOGUE, AND A WRITER AND BROADCASTER.

Jesus is stripped of his garments

Timothy Radcliffe

We take off our clothes to wash or to prepare for sleep. This is quite different from having them torn from us by force. A friend of mine, going through immigration control in a rough part of the world, made the mistake of showing his irritation. He was stripped and searched. This was a ritual of humiliation, such as Jesus endured.

We claim an identity by the clothes that we choose to wear. People's good pride is undermined when they are forced to wear clothes they would not choose, as when the Nazis forced Jews and gay people to wear specially coloured stars. And if our clothes are stripped from us, then we lose face and more. We are unprotected before the gaze of others, leaving us feeling disempowered and vulnerable. The media often strip people naked on their pages, exposing their failures and weaknesses. We will all have known moments of shame when we are shown up, with our little secrets unveiled. We are seen as we are, and fear that we shall not be loved.

After the fall Adam and Eve hid in the bushes from the sight of God. How could God love them after they had grabbed the forbidden fruit? But God has compassion on them and gives them skins. This was just a foretaste of God's deeper kindness when, in Jesus, our own shame is embraced and God is stripped and then left naked on the cross.

When the early Christians came to baptism, the bishop would shout out: 'Off with your clothes.' They stripped for immersion in the waters of baptism. There is no need for any shame. Gregory of Nyssa wrote: 'Casting off these fading leaves which veil our lives we should once again present ourselves before the eyes of our Maker'.

This means that we too can throw away our 'fig leaves'. We need no disguises to gain God's love. We do not need to claim status by broadcasting our achievements, or making absurd claims to self-importance. We do not need to project an impressive facade, or be propped up by others admiration. In the words of a fourth century prayer: 'Unveil our eyes, give us confidence, do not let us be ashamed or embarrassed, do not let us despise ourselves.' Jesus has been stripped. We need not fear to be naked. We are loved as we are.

FR TIMOTHY RADCLIFFE WAS MASTER OF THE DOMINICAN ORDER. HE IS THE WINNER OF THE 2007 MICHAEL RAMSEY PRIZE FOR THEOLOGICAL WRITING FOR HIS BOOK *WHAT IS THE POINT OF BEING A CHRISTIAN?* AND IS THE AUTHOR OF THE ARCHBISHOP OF CANTERBURY'S 2009 LENT BOOK *WHY GO TO CHURCH?*

Jesus is nailed to the cross

Ann Widdecombe

One of Our Lord's greatest mental agonies on the cross must have been seeing how let down everyone around him felt. He knew that this was not the end but his mother, disciples and followers thought it was and he had to cause them disappointment and distress in order to do what was right. He would have watched his mother watching him, and known that he had the power to come down from the cross and turn her sorrow to joy but that he must not: there was a much greater cause to serve.

Sometimes we have to find the courage to let other people down, even our nearest and dearest because we know that what we are doing is right. A student who has received the best and most expensive education may have to say to his parents that he is not following his father into the City but is going to work in the Third World, or a politician may have to disappoint loyal supporters by espousing a cause they do not believe in, or a daughter resist an arranged marriage the parents have set their hearts on.

In so many ways, big and small, we undergo conflicts of loyalty in which we know someone we love or respect will feel let down. Our Lord showed us this path in his most agonising moments.

THE RIGHT HONOURABLE ANN WIDDECOMBE IS A FORMER MEMBER OF PARLIAMENT, AND A NOVELIST. SHE WAS MP FOR MAIDSTONE FROM 1987 TO 1997 AND FOR MAIDSTONE AND THE WEALD FROM 1997 TO 2010. SINCE 2002 SHE HAS MADE NUMEROUS TELEVISION AND RADIO APPEARANCES.

Jesus is crucified

Robin Baird-Smith

There is an essential ambiguity in the last words of Jesus from the cross, 'My God, my God, why hast thou forsaken me?' We are accustomed in modern western culture to treat such sentiments as automatically defeatist. This must be the cry of despair we feel. This is no doubt why Albert Camus once wrote, 'How can I subscribe to a religion when the central image is a punctured, deflated human being pinned to two pieces of wood with nails.'

But I believe this is to misunderstand an essential element in Jewish psychology. To the Jewish believer, the relationship between man and God is an argument, a running battle. Job shakes his fist at heaven. God shouts back, 'Answer thou me'. The image of Gentle Jesus meek and mild may be very appealing to many. Not to me. Look at the image of Jesus in Pasolini's brilliant film *The Gospel According to St Matthew*. Here, Jesus is a quick tempered human being with volatile emotions – full of insatiable love for humanity but turning in an instant to anger. In fact the two are not incompatible.

As a young man attending the synagogue, Jesus would have been brought up into the tradition of argument and dispute. The Jews arrive at the truth by disputing about interpretation of the Torah. They argue their heads off even to this day. This was Jesus' world.

On the cross then, when he exclaims, 'Why has thou forsaken me?' there is here more than meets the eye. Despair maybe, but also the expression of anger. The repression of anger, as the psychologists tell us emphatically, results in depression, despair.

And one thing all theologians agree about is that though Jesus was divine – he was also truly human. As St Paul tells us in the Epistle to the Philippians, God emptied himself to become man.

Robin Baird-Smith is a Publisher, and a Director of *The Tablet*. His wife and middle child were killed in a car accident in 1994.

THE THIRTEENTH STATION

Jesus is taken down from the cross

Margaret Mizen

Mary was at the foot of the Cross. As Jesus was taken down from it, she was confronted with the death of her beloved son. When I arrived at the place where Jimmy was dying I was confronted by the reality that something really bad had happened; I think I knew then that he was dead, even before it was confirmed.

The day Jimmy died, many people came to our house. Although I was so grateful for people supporting us, I was overwhelmed at the response. During the evening I sought sanctuary in my bedroom and just lay on the bed.

Lying down I was struck by thoughts of Mary at the foot of the Cross. I'd watched my son Tommy cradling Jimmy in his arms as he died. I had such a sense of the pain, both mentally and physically, that Mary must have felt. At the same time, a tiny part of me was experiencing a comfort and joy, I was so aware of a voice, 'Jimmy is safe. He is with me'. I didn't know what to make of it, but that sense of Jimmy being in Heaven, with Jesus, has stayed with me. To this day I believe my son was taken for a reason, I don't know what that reason is, but maybe Jimmy has become a focus for young people. I often ask for the intercession of my beautiful son for all young people, growing in a world that has become so used to violence, to work for Peace.

On New Year's Day, of the year Jimmy died, two girls who were fellow students were killed in a car crash. The entire year group, including Jimmy, attended both the funerals. We were told after Jimmy died that all the students had spent much time discussing their own mortalities. They all asked what their funerals would look like, and what they would like people to say about them after their deaths. Jimmy had said he 'just wanted to be remembered.'

Lord, I thank you for the gift of Jimmy. Thank you for the joy he brought to all who knew him. May his life and witness give hope to all our precious young people. Amen.

MARGARET MIZEN'S SON, JIMMY, WAS KILLED IN AN UNPROVOKED ATTACK IN A BAKER'S SHOP CLOSE TO THE FAMILY HOME IN SOUTH EAST LONDON, ON SATURDAY, 10 MAY 2008, THE DAY AFTER HIS 16TH BIRTHDAY.

Jesus' body is laid in the tomb

Rachel Denton

The body of a dead person becomes a non-person very quickly. A friend once told me that, at the moment of his father dying, although the physical change was very slight, the sense of 'who' he was left his body very quickly, and it became a 'what', a thing.

When I think of the people that I am tempted to turn into a 'what' rather than a 'who', homeless people figure highly. Their obvious poverty troubles me; the limit of what I am able, prepared, to offer them accuses me. It is easier to bury them outside of my life-zone: 'the homeless', a thing to be dealt with, a dilemma, a problem, a sense of unease. It is easier to roll the stone into place.

Recently, I was walking through Lincoln with another friend. We came across a young woman on the street, quietly asking for money. We gave her a little, with a word or two of conversation about street-life. As we were moving on she surprised us both by taking hold of my friend's hand and asking if she could give him a hug. My friend hesitated: the woman was dirty, smelly, possibly inebriated; we were dressed for a celebratory meal. Then with a wry grimace towards me, ever so gently, he bent down and held her briefly. Her request, his response, my inclusion in it: whose was the gift?

If we dare to admit someone else's humanity, we risk the possibility that they might ask for more than we are prepared to give.

If we dare to admit someone else's humanity, we risk the possibility that they might want to give us more than we are prepared to accept.

It is safer to roll the stone into place, and to walk away.

Rachel Denton is a Catholic hermit in the Nottinghamshire Diocese. She writes for Redemptorist Publications. In 2009 she took to the fourth plinth in Trafalgar Square for Antony Gormley's *One and Other*.

The Stations of the
Resurrection

Jesus rises from the dead (Matthew 28.1-7)

Wendy Beckett

When we make the Stations of the Cross, we are grieving with Jesus and expressing our gratitude to him. Because of his love he gladly died for us. But with the Stations of the Resurrection, it is all joy as well as gratitude.

Jesus *was* crucified, but he *is* risen. The Resurrection is not in the past, it is in the present. This is the Jesus we meet in the Sacraments. This Jesus truly died, went into death and came out of it, into a fullness of life that we cannot imagine. What artist could portray this? To me the truest image of our risen saviour is precisely this, the empty tomb. The tomb proclaims the reality of his death: this is what he did for us. The emptiness proclaims the reality of his Resurrection:

this is what he is for us. How it happened we do not know, but that it happened is the foundation of our faith. Everything Jesus does, he does for us. The Epistle to the Hebrews calls Him 'our pioneer'. He went into death and came through into glory so that we could do the same. His Resurrection is the certain promise of our Resurrection. The Resurrection of Jesus is our deepest reason for hope. None of those we have lost to death are really lost. In this life we cannot see them with our earthly eyes or hear from them with our ears, just as we cannot see or hear Jesus. But they are as alive as he is alive, and all sorrow will be swept away in the joy of heaven. The emptiness of the tomb, its silence and vacancy, is an image of the life of faith, which may have no visible signs of the reality of God (this is the common experience though there are exceptions). We look into the emptiness and say: I believe.

Dear Jesus, may we be happy to live with the emptiness, secure in our faith that it is only a sign of the glorious fullness in which you live eternally.

SISTER WENDY BECKETT IS A CONTEMPLATIVE HERMIT AND ART HISTORIAN. SHE HAS PRESENTED A NUMBER OF

ART PROGRAMMES FOR THE BBC AND CONTINUES TO MAKE TELEVISION APPEARANCES. SHE IS AUTHOR OF NUMEROUS BOOKS ABOUT RELIGIOUS ART.

Peter and John arrive at the empty tomb (John 20.1-9)

Russell Stannard

For most people empty space is synonymous with nothingness or absence. But that is not how physicists see it.

Consider the distant galaxies of stars. They are still receding from each other in the aftermath of the Big Bang. Recently it was found that they are not slowing down under the effect of their mutual gravity, as had previously been supposed. Instead they are accelerating away from each other. This is because the space between them – so-called empty space – is filled with a special kind of energy, and this energy exerts a hitherto unrecognised repulsive anti-gravity force.

So, space is not nothing. It is a mysterious something filled with energy. It is called dark energy. 'Dark' because it cannot be seen. Why is it invisible? For something to be visible, a chair for example, it must have a finite size and occupy a particular location in space. We are able to point to it and say, 'that is what I am talking about.' But when it comes to dark energy, where does one point? It is everywhere.

The disciples found the tomb empty. They saw no body. It had been through his physical body they had previously seen and known him – a body occupying a particular location (like the chair) – but one that was necessarily absent elsewhere. Jesus had now shed such physical limitations in order that he might be found everywhere. This necessarily meant that, like the dark energy, he was no longer to be seen.

So, how are we to know of this all-pervading presence? In the same way as we know about the all-pervading presence of dark energy. Though it is itself invisible, we see the effects it produces on that which we do see – the motion of the galaxies. Likewise, Jesus now makes his presence felt in the way he influences the lives and thinking of his followers.

Peter and John arrive at the empty tomb (John 20.1-9)

RUSSELL STANNARD OBE IS EMERITUS PROFESSOR OF PHYSICS AT THE OPEN UNIVERSITY AND A LICENSED LAY MINISTER IN THE CHURCH OF ENGLAND. HE HAS WRITTEN EXTENSIVELY ON SCIENCE AND RELIGION FOR ADULTS AND CHILDREN.

The risen Lord appears to Mary Magdalen (John 20: 11-16)

Siri Abrahamson

Alone outside the tomb where Jesus' body no longer lay was Mary Magdalen. The Gospel tells us she was crying, and how could she not be? 'They have taken my Lord away,' she says. I feel for Mary; for her grief, for her loneliness, for her incomprehension. 'They have taken my Lord away, and I don't know where they have put him' (John 20:13). Mary Magdalen was a close friend of Jesus. She was at the cross when all but one of the male disciples had fled. She had been at Jesus' burial. And as she stood weeping outside the empty tomb, she became the first person to see Jesus after his Resurrection.

When her despair was so great that all she could do was stand and weep, Christ came to her – quite literally. When my despair was boundless, he made himself known to me too. Our second daughter died during labour. As I lay in the hospital bed, I kissed her beautiful face and clutched her still-warm body, tenderly wrapped in a hospital blanket, and I thought my heart would rend in two. There was no Christ in our lives, no faith, no religion, to offer my husband and me any consolation. We did not know how or where we would find the strength to cope with our grief and carry on. I am still not entirely sure of the answer. But this I do know: we were asked about having our daughter blessed. We said yes. The hospital priest came and said a prayer. And then, as we held our baby girl on that January afternoon, a shaft of light came through the window. It was the first ray of sunshine in many winter weeks. Cynics and non-believers would say we were clutching at straws. I don't care. Neither I would guess did Mary; she knew she had seen the risen Christ, and ran to tell the other disciples. Many grey and gloomy and heart-breaking weeks followed that day in the hospital. The day of Elspeth's funeral the skies were heavy and dark. Following the service, just as we walked out of the chapel, a bright, brilliant ray of sunshine suddenly penetrated the clouds.

Jesus doesn't take Mary Magdalen's sorrow or pain away. She is not allowed to hold him close or spend much time with him. Still – he makes his presence known. For me, those unexpected rays of light were of comfort, filling me with peace and hope, and leading me in time on my own journey of faith.

SIRI ABRAHAMSON AND HER HUSBAND, JUSTIN PORTESS, WERE DRAWN TO THE CATHOLIC CHURCH AND BEGAN ATTENDING ST JOHN THE EVANGELIST IN ISLINGTON FOLLOWING THE DEATH OF THEIR DAUGHTER, ELSPETH. THEY COMPLETED THE RITE OF CHRISTIAN INITIATION OF ADULTS (RCIA) AND WERE RECEIVED INTO THE CATHOLIC CHURCH ON HOLY SATURDAY, 2011.

Jesus appears to two disciples on the road to Emmaus (Luke 24.13-28)

Marie Collins

We can imagine the feelings of those two disciples heading away from Jerusalem on the road to Emmaus. We can imagine their despair and disillusionment at the events of Good Friday; they had left Jerusalem feeling abandoned and fearful, the certainties and hope in their life replaced by confusion and doubt.

When I realised that the leaders of my Church had put the protection of their institution before their moral duty to keep children safe and to care for those who had been grievously hurt by their ministers, I felt utter despair and disillusionment. I felt abandoned by the Church that had been the one certainty in my life. I could not bring myself to enter a church: these buildings were just hollow reminders of the past, they reminded me of what was lost, they had no meaning for me.

I headed away from my religious practice into the unknown, as those disciples had headed away from Jerusalem. I was on an unfamiliar road with no signposts. From the time of being told as a small child, on entering my local church, that I was in 'God's house', this was where my God was present. My belief had always been expressed by attending my church and following the rituals. Now that this was lost, what had I got? Where was I going?

Standing on a beach alone one day, watching the waves crash on the shore, I struggled with these thoughts. My faith in God had not changed; I was surrounded by his wonderful creation. I felt him all around me. I knew then that whatever the future would hold I would not be alone on my journey; Christ was with me as he had been with those disciples on the road to Emmaus.

Jesus appears to two disciples on the road to Emmaus (Luke 24.13-28)

MARIE COLLINS IS A PRACTISING CATHOLIC AND CLERICAL ABUSE SURVIVOR. SHE HAS CAMPAIGNED FOR JUSTICE FOR SURVIVORS FOR MANY YEARS AND RECEIVED THE HUMBERT AWARD FOR COURAGE IN 2010 FOR THIS WORK. IN FEBRUARY 2012 SHE ADDRESSED AN INTERNATIONAL SYMPOSIUM IN ROME ON CHILD ABUSE, *TOWARDS HEALING AND RENEWAL*.

The risen Lord is recognised in the breaking of bread (Luke 24.28-35)

Antony Feltham-White

A s they ate their supper together at the end of a tiring day, the travellers on the road to Emmaus were suddenly able to recognise the extraordinary in the ordinary. Their mysterious companion had been Jesus himself! On deployment with the military the extraordinary becomes commonplace and finding Christ in the fast-moving and frightening environment of a twenty-first century battlefield can be a challenge.

However, there are certain similarities. Travelling on foot limits your luggage: you can only take what you can comfortably carry. That's true if you're journeying to Emmaus or deploying on a military operation overseas. The less you have to occupy your time, the more you notice your surroundings. The travellers on the road were able to listen afresh to the scriptures, unencumbered by the realities of their normal everyday existence.

As a parish priest I often considered my role as being akin to running a petrol station. My parishioners would stop in once a week to fill up their tanks. I'd send them off with a cheery wave, hoping their journeys would not throw up anything unexpected. Sometimes I'd see them out and about, sometimes I wouldn't. I rarely travelled anywhere with them.

As a military chaplain my whole focus is on the journey. I travel everywhere with the soldiers of whichever unit I am attached to. At times I depend on them to keep me alive, likewise there are times when they rely on me. Together we try to find the ordinary in the extraordinary. It protects our sanity.

A military chaplain is more a simple signpost than a pump attendant, pointing to what is ordinary and familiar in an unfamiliar and potentially lethal environment. To do that with any success it is essential to look for Jesus in all we do and wherever we go. Taking time to look for Christ in our surroundings ensures our focus is on something

The risen Lord is recognised in the breaking of bread (Luke 24.28-35)

familiar and comforting, no matter how unfamiliar or dangerous the situation.

I remember standing in a Battalion aid post watching a young army doctor and her team working on a soldier who had been shot in the head. I suspect he had died before he hit the ground, yet the medical team did everything they could with great care and commitment. All the time she worked the doctor looked at me with little, almost imperceptible, shakes of her head. After a period of time, I can't say how long, the urgency of action slowed and there were tears. Looking back I recall the love and professional attention the medical team gave to this young soldier. In the inhumanity of the situation I witnessed great humanity. So often I have found that where there is great darkness there is also light. No matter where our life-journey takes us there will always be the opportunity to find the extraordinary in the ordinary if we focus first on finding Jesus Christ.

THE REVEREND ANTONY FELTHAM-WHITE IS AN ARMY CHAPLAIN. HE HAS SERVED IN IRAQ AND AFGHANISTAN, MOST RECENTLY IN 2011 WITH THE 2ND BATTALION THE PARACHUTE REGIMENT.

The risen Lord appears to his disciples in a locked room (John 20.19-21; Luke 24.36-43)

Vincent Nichols

The words in St John's Gospel describing the moment are terse and vivid: 'The doors were shut for fear'; 'It was late'; 'The first day of the week'; 'Jesus stood among them'; 'Peace be with you'; 'He showed them his hands and his side'.

Fear had shut the door: fear of what might happen; fear that they might be next; fear of an unwelcome knock, an unwanted visitor. Fears such as those can grip the insides of all of us, riddled as we are with uncertainty.

Jesus didn't knock. He simply came and 'stood among them'. That's how it often is; in the worst moments, he simply turns up, at our side. It might be at a night time hour or in a few moments of stillness in a busy day. The risen Lord has that capacity: to be with us, each one of us, as and when he wishes, to bring us his grace.

'Peace be with you'. That is his grace; an inner peace which the world cannot give. This is the supreme gift, a gift so hard to embrace fully, so difficult to grasp in the welter of worries that assail us, that are often self-generated! This precious gift confirms our dignity as sons and daughters of God, knowing that our lives are in the hands of our loving Father.

But the next words are so crucial 'He showed them his hands and side'.

The Lord's gift of peace does not excuse us from the pain of living. We all bear some share in those wounds, for we all live in a world fractured by sin. But the message of our risen Lord is that his gift of inner peace – a promise of heaven – is stronger than every wound.

Indeed, from his wounds flow the Blood by which that peace is won.

Deep in thy wounds, Lord, hide and shelter me.

The risen Lord appears to his disciples in a locked room

HIS GRACE THE MOST REVEREND VINCENT NICHOLS IS THE ARCHBISHOP OF WESTMINSTER, PRESIDENT OF THE CATHOLIC BISHOPS' CONFERENCE OF ENGLAND AND WALES, AND HEAD OF THE ROMAN CATHOLIC CHURCH IN ENGLAND AND WALES.

Jesus gives the power to forgive sins (John 20.20-23)

Kelly Connor

The risen Christ entered the locked room where the frightened disciples were taking refuge and calmed them by saying, 'Peace be with you.' Moments later he repeated the same words, this time to calm their overflowing joy. 'After saying this he breathed on them and said: Receive the Holy Spirit. If you forgive anyone's sins, they are forgiven.'

The disciples' response isn't recorded, but I imagine them questioning whether their behaviour during the arrest and crucifixion of Christ was forgivable, and forgiven. Of course they were forgiven, you might exclaim, and I agree, but that isn't what I'm referring to. I'm thinking of the difficulty of accepting forgiveness when our actions, whether intentional or not, cause extreme hurt, or even death.

At age 17, when driving to work on a quiet Sunday morning in 1971, I collided with an elderly woman who was three-quarters of the way across the road on a pedestrian crossing. I saw her for only a split-second before hitting her. I was speeding and looking in the rear view mirror at the car behind me. She tried to outrun me, but couldn't.

Margaret Healy died a violent death for which I was wholly responsible. Her family immediately forgave me but, engulfed by guilt and shame, I shunned their generosity. I was haunted by the question, 'Do I have the right to live now that I have caused a death?'. My family fractured under the stress and never recovered. It took three decades to understand my destiny and to reclaim my self-worth and my identity.

In 2004, I published my memoir, *To Cause a Death*. Following a radio interview, one mother, whose young daughter died after running in front of a car, contacted me. As she spoke, I braced myself, expecting condemnation, but instead she told me that every day for ten years since her daughter's death she has worried about the driver.

Her gentle voice reminded me that people have always been more forgiving of me than I have of myself. It took a long time to realise that when Christ says we can forgive 'anyone' their sins, that includes self-forgiveness.

Only after forgiving myself could I finally accept forgiveness from others. And only then could I hear the words of the risen Christ, 'Peace be with you.'

KELLY CONNOR IS AN AUSTRALIAN AUTHOR, NOVELIST, PLAYWRIGHT AND PUBLIC SPEAKER. SHE GIVES TALKS AND WORKSHOPS IN PRISONS ON BEHALF OF THE FORGIVENESS PROJECT.

The risen Lord confirms the faith of Thomas (John 20.24-29)

Anne Maguire

Thomas put his fingers in the wound on Christ's side. He wouldn't believe until he had. I didn't ask to put my fingers into that wound. I believed. I thought my faith was strong. But Jesus took my hand; he placed it in his side and held it there. He showed me how strong my faith is.

I feel like I've walked the Way of the Cross with Our Lady, watching Jesus being stripped. My children lost everything: their home, their parents for ten years; their possessions, people who were supposed to be friends helped themselves. I thank God the children all have that bit of Christian faith in them. They respect the Church and have brought up their children in the faith. Despite everything that's happened, they still have that. Faith is the only thing that can't be taken from you, no matter what.

My father was a good man and always said, 'As long as you keep believing you'll get through life. You will be tested by things. You might have friends who turn their back on you, but don't let that dishearten you. In the end they'll see you for the good person you are'. When I was in prison I used to think a lot about my family; my parents and my children. I carried my cross with strong faith. I could have given up, but God wouldn't let me. I fought with him; 'Why are you letting this happen to me? What did I do that was so wrong that I deserve this?' But I never gave up my faith. Not when they insulted me and beat me during my interrogation; not when the police beat my boys; not when we were wrongfully imprisoned. I always believed in God. We spent a long time together in my cell. One day I was looking at the picture of the Sacred Heart that I had, and I said to God, 'Okay, it's you and me against the nation,' because that's how it felt. My husband had served in the British Army. We had lived in London as man and wife for seventeen years and had four children. We worked hard, but the country had turned its back on us. 'You bring me through this,' I said to God, 'please send someone in authority to bring our case to light'. Then Cardinal Hume came along. I know I served the time and God made me and the family go through it all. But in the end he sent that person. Cardinal Hume was the one who helped us to prove our innocence. I knew God would send someone. I had faith in him, and he had faith in me.

IN 2005 PRIME MINISTER TONY BLAIR ISSUED A PUBLIC APOLOGY TO THE MAGUIRE SEVEN AND THE GUILDFORD FOUR FOR THE MISCARRIAGES OF JUSTICE THEY HAD SUFFERED. THREE DAYS BEFORE HE DIED, POPE JOHN PAUL II BESTOWED ON **ANNE MAGUIRE** THE BENEMERENTI MEDAL, IN RECOGNITION OF HER 'REMARKABLE ABILITY TO FORGIVE' AND FOR HER WORK FOR HER PARISH, HER FAMILY AND HER COMMUNITY.

THE TWENTY THIRD STATION

The risen Lord meets his disciples on the shore of Galilee (John 21.4-14)

Lucy Russell

How do you measure success? A good degree? Where you are on the career ladder? What you have in your bank account? Does this kind of 'success' actually make us happy? We live in a society which encourages long working hours and the pursuit of higher incomes, but once you reach a certain level, money does not really bring happiness. What matters more say the psychologists, is having one intimate, emotional relationship. A brilliant career and financial security cannot on their own bring happiness and contentment, and isn't that a better measure of success? When in October 2011 anti-Capitalist protesters set up camp outside St Paul's Cathedral in London, commentators asked what Jesus would say. Where would he be? Camping outside in the cold, speaking out against inequality, or inside the religious building worrying about lost revenue from visitors and their health and safety? Before his death and Resurrection he would perhaps have been in the camp. But a post-Resurrection Jesus might be standing back from the action slightly, watching and waiting. Looking to see what his disciples had learned.

With God everything is possible. The disciples were out fishing alone all night. They caught nothing. Then Jesus arrived for breakfast; he told them to cast out their nets and they were filled. The disciples had been waiting all night to catch something, and now success! The nets were full! But this is not what actually made the night a success. The fish were a sign of success – a signal of something else: the presence of God. Peter jumps out of the boat and goes to where he wants to be. His interest lies with the person on the beach, not with the fish in the nets. He makes his way to the beach as quickly as possible to be with the person who means most to him. For the commentators discussing the anti-Capitalist protest the question might become what would St Peter do, where would our first Pope be? He would perhaps be walking away from the city of London; abandoning the wealth he had accrued to pursue his personal relationship with Christ. On the beach with his friends and the person he loved, Peter shared the fish for breakfast. Is there any point in filling our nets without friends to share our catch with? It is Peter's friendship with Jesus that leads to a successful catch.

We achieve success when we invest in our relationships with one another and with God, with whom we are all invited to have an intimate relationship.

DR LUCY RUSSELL IS THE AUTHOR OF TWO EDUCATION TITLES PUBLISHED BY CONTINUUM AND A FREELANCE WRITER. HER WORK HAS APPEARED IN *THE UNIVERSE* AND *THE CATHOLIC HERALD*. SHE MAKES REGULAR CONTRIBUTIONS TO *FAITH TODAY*, AND *SUNDAY PLUS*.

The risen Lord appoints Peter the Head of the Church (John 21.15-22)

Peter Stanford

I've always been drawn to Saint Peter. You don't come across many Peters anymore. It is one of those Christian names that has fallen dramatically out of fashion, though the fact that we share it isn't reason enough on its own to make me feel comforted by his proximity. That runs deeper.

Here is Peter, of all the apostles the one who is closest to Jesus, someone who works next to him, who loves him dearly, who knows him more thoroughly than we can ever hope to, who has witnessed the miracles he has performed, and who has listened to every remarkable word he has said, words that we can only read on a page, and then just a fraction of those he spoke. Yet, here too is Peter, the man who betrays Jesus three times as the cock crows.

With all his advantages, Peter fails Jesus. What hope is there for us?

Well, for me, he represents that hope. Despite all his shortcomings – or, perhaps, because of them – Peter is given the keys to the Kingdom of Heaven and has primacy conferred on him by the risen Lord. His example should reassure us that we will still be loved by God at the end of it all, even if we make the most terrible mistakes, lack faith, or are overcome by our human weakness. How extraordinary is that?

Jesus' trust in the flawed Peter, his command to his apostle three times to 'feed my sheep' (John 21.17), suggests something about the frailty and the value in God's eyes of all believers, whether today they be in the back row of the pews, or sit on Saint Peter's throne. We are as one. There is then something very democratic about the flaws that we share with Jesus' chosen apostle.

And his example speaks to me also of the value of persevering. An earlier generation used to pray for 'final perseverance'. When I was younger that sounded odd, a kind of abdication, but the older I get the more I know what it is my parents and grandparents were seeking with that request. Peter is the symbol of human perseverance.

PETER STANFORD IS AN AUTHOR, BROADCASTER AND BIOGRAPHER. A FORMER EDITOR OF THE *CATHOLIC HERALD*, HE WRITES FOR *THE DAILY TELEGRAPH*, *THE INDEPENDENT ON SUNDAY* AND *THE OBSERVER*, AND HAS A REGULAR COLUMN IN *THE TABLET*.

THE TWENTY FIFTH STATION

The risen Lord sends His disciples to evangelise all nations (Matthew 28.18-20)

Bernard Longley

As today's disciples we can see ourselves in this Station, receiving our mandate from the risen Lord to 'go out to the whole world and proclaim the Good News' (Mark 16:15). It seems a daunting mission to us even today when almost one third of the world's population are baptised followers of Christ. It must have appeared an impossible task, humanly speaking, to the little band of disciples who formed the early Church.

It is the Resurrection of the Lord that makes all the difference, along with his paschal gift of the Holy Spirit. In the light of his own rising from the dead all things seem possible. In our own day we are sent, in the power of the Holy Spirit, to bring the Gospel message to the ends of the earth.

That is why, despite all the challenges and obstacles along the way, I feel confident about the task entrusted to our generation to work for the unity of the Church, alongside baptised brothers and sisters of other Churches and ecclesial communities. We have been sent to bring the Good News together and we must find fresh patterns of evangelising together.

This common mission is one of the goals of ecumenism and it strengthens the hope of all the members of the Anglican-Roman Catholic International Commission, whose third phase of work I have been appointed to co-chair alongside Archbishop David Moxon from New Zealand. Anglicans and Catholics need to find new ways of responding together to the risen Lord's commission.

As Pope Benedict inaugurates a Year of Faith in 2012, we find renewed confidence, through the Holy Spirit, for the task of the new evangelisation entrusted to us. Our understanding of the men and women, the interests and cultures of our own time must help us find new ways of making the message of Jesus Christ, always the same and ever-new, available to our society.

May the risen Lord enable us to open the gateway to faith.

HIS GRACE THE MOST REVEREND BERNARD LONGLEY IS ARCHBISHOP OF BIRMINGHAM.

THE TWENTY SIXTH STATION

The risen Lord ascends to the Father (Acts 1.6-11)

John Sentamu

Facing big changes in our lives can be deeply scary. And in life, there are changes we choose and also changes which are thrust upon us, whether we like it or not.

I had a major change when I had to leave Uganda and came to England in 1974. It was very hard to leave all that had been familiar and start a radically new life here. Yet, in retrospect, it was the turning point which led me to where I am today.

So I am sure that the disciples felt bereft on Ascension Day when they saw their beloved Lord taken from their sight into heaven. Just forty days after his Resurrection, their Lord had been taken from them again. Yet their experience of the physicality of the Resurrection of Christ told them that this was not the end.

They were right! At Pentecost, God would send his Holy Spirit upon them, freeing them from fear, so that they could boldly proclaim the good news that Jesus had risen from the dead and ascended to his Father and their Father.

Ascension Day made all this possible. It is the glorious climax of Jesus' time on earth for he had accomplished everything which his coming in our human flesh had done. All was 'finished'. On Ascension Day, Jesus brought all our humanity before the life of the Glorious Trinity as he was glorified. The risen Christ of earth is the Christ of Heaven saving us to the utmost. Death therefore ushers us, not into oblivion but into his near-presence.

During his earthly life, Jesus, like us, was limited to one time and one place. But on Ascension Day, the risen Jesus is glorified by God the Father to be the Christ of all time and in all places so that he is with us wherever we are and whatever we may be doing.

Knowing that the risen, ascended and glorified Jesus stands beside us in all times and places, helps us to embrace change without fear. Remember that change often makes new things possible as it helps us to grow and flourish.

So don't be afraid but be the person whom our risen Lord Jesus is calling you to be!

THE MOST REVEREND AND RIGHT HONOURABLE DR JOHN SENTAMU IS ARCHBISHOP OF YORK.

Mary and the apostles pray for the coming of the Holy Spirit (Acts 1.12-14)

Ruth Burrows

'There appeared to them parted tongues as it were of fire, and it sat upon every one of them; and they were all filled with the Holy Spirit...' (Acts 2.3-4)

This divine gift, without which there would be no revelation, no holiness, no Church, found hearts ready to receive it, and none so ready as the heart of Mary. To so much as glimpse what it means to be a disciple of Jesus, means longing ardently for the living flame of love to sear through our selfishness and superficiality, to wrest the heart of stone from our bodies and to give us instead the heart of Christ. To be a Christian means making Christ present in the world. For each one of us this is our primary witness.

It cannot become a reality unless we bend our whole being to receive the loving intimacy Jesus offers us: 'I no longer call you servants but friends' (John 15:15). It demands sustained, arduous effort, a firm commitment to enthrone him as sole king of our hearts. The whole of our life, our activities, our relationships, our thinking and speaking, all must be directed towards union with him. Only when we evangelise our own hearts and minds will what we say, proclaim and preach, draw the men and women of our country to turn to their Saviour. Scripture gives us our blessed Lady as the model of the true disciple, showing us her life totally, absolutely dedicated to Jesus her Son.

'Blessed the womb that bore you and the breasts that fed you!' (Luke 11.27), was a woman's spontaneous exclamation at the splendour of the human Jesus. Jesus did not deny his mother's blessedness in this, but declared her more blessed for really hearing the word of God and obeying it.

A private, intimate communication of the Holy Spirit to the disciples had occurred on Easter Day. The event of Pentecost was a public theophany attended by tangible phenomena: a mighty wind surging through the house, and what seemed like tongues of fire settling on the heads of each person present. It was a manifestation of the birth of the Church and, for the mother of Jesus, entry into the fullness of her divine motherhood.

She will show us what it means to abide in Jesus, to live in him, to be so one with him that our prayer to the Father is the prayer of Jesus himself, and the fire of love that Jesus died to enkindle on earth, will burn within us. We will then know the peace of Jesus, peace beyond normal understanding, peace which nothing temporal and earthly can destroy, the peace and joy of the Eternal Word, Son of Mary and our Brother.

RUTH BURROWS IS A CARMELITE NUN FROM QUIDENHAM IN NORFOLK. SHE IS THE AUTHOR OF A NUMBER OF BESTSELLING BOOKS INCLUDING *LOVE UNKNOWN*, THE ARCHBISHOP OF CANTERBURY'S LENT BOOK FOR 2012.

Jesus sends the promised Holy Spirit on Mary and the apostles (Acts 2.1-8)

Paschal Uche

He was clearly a man saturated in hours of prayer both gentle and generous. This was the lasting impression of my brief encounter with the Holy Father as I welcomed him on behalf of young Catholics.

Later, as I stood in Hyde Park surrounded by thousands, one young person said to me, 'I have never seen so many young people in the Church.' What an encouragement for her faith, I thought. Perhaps as a young person she was all too familiar with the many young people who are confirmed out of the church rather than in it, with those left behind, feeling a sense of being alone. That should never be, because the Lord has sent us the Holy Spirit precisely as a promise and proof that his presence will never leave or forsake us. The Disciples and our Blessed Mother in the upper room were few in number; it was the gift of the Holy Spirit that gave them comfort, courage and power to live and spread the good news. The Papal visit showed we are actually many in number but more importantly, no matter how many or how few, we are one body, one spirit in Christ. It is the gift of the Holy Spirit that unites and empowers us for mission; a mission to renew the face of the earth through loving service.

Pope Benedict in his address to the youth said we were made from love for love, and God who is love desires our holiness: the perfection of love. In essence the Spirit is being sent to make you and me saints. May the Lord first fill the hearts of the faithful before he fills the pews of our churches so that, enkindled with the fire of his love, he might renew the face of our hungry, thirsty and troubled world through you and me.

PASCHAL UCHE WELCOMED POPE BENEDICT XVI ON BEHALF OF BRITAIN'S YOUNG CATHOLICS AT WESTMINSTER CATHEDRAL DURING THE 2010 PAPAL VISIT. HIS SPEECH WAS HEARD AND SEEN BY MILLIONS AROUND THE WORLD.

AFTERWORD

Our personal reflections, brought together as a collection, are the thoughts and prayers of a community. Community, which comes with a sense of being welcomed and accepted, is one of the most wonderful aspects of being part of a 'Church'. What faith gives us is not only a sense of belonging, but a sense of being. It is who we are. But it isn't always easy. Dennis Potter said, 'Religion to me has always been the wound, not the bandage.' Doubt is part of faith. Speaking at Canterbury Cathedral in September 2011 in conversation with the Archbishop of Canterbury Dr Rowan Williams, Frank Skinner said:

> Most of my conversations are with atheists, who say how can anyone with any kind of brain believe in God in 2011? How can you be so sure? And my point is, I'm not sure and in fact I think faith, that kind of complete and utter blind faith, is a very dangerous thing. I see myself as a person of doubt, and I think doubt is absolutely at the centre of being a human being, and is important. I worry when I hear religious people who have no doubt,

just fundamentalist beliefs, and I worry when
I hear atheists who seem to have no doubt
at all. I think that that is an essential part of
being a human being.

Many of us have days when we think, what if we have
got it all wrong? What if there is nothing after all? Even
Mother Teresa experienced a crisis of faith. She wrote
to Reverend Michael Van Der Peet on one occasion in
September 1979, 'Jesus has a very special love for you.
As for me, the silence and the emptiness is so great
that I look and do not see, listen and do not hear.' In
truth we are all, as the Archbishop of Westminster
notes in his meditation, riddled with uncertainty.

But our uncertainty doesn't make us any less worthy.
Anyone can write their own meditations on the
Stations, although it can be a personal challenge. We
are all changed and shaped by the events which happen
in our lives. They become part of our story, but some
of us are grappling with very difficult stories. Dr John
Sentamu says that facing big changes in our lives can
be scary, but we shouldn't be afraid to be the person
the risen Christ is calling us to be. So it is with writing
personal meditations: it can be daunting, it is a process
that strips us and leave us feeling exposed. The first
time that, as a Parish, we wrote our own Stations and

read them aloud during a public devotion, many of us struggled to read our own contribution, feeling that it was not as well written or as poignant as others. Feelings of 'unworthiness' are familiar to us all. Some of the very well-known authors, actors, broadcasters and peers whom I approached to write a Station for this collection declined because they didn't feel they could do it: they weren't 'holy' enough, they couldn't write with the certainty of other contributors. None of us is worthy of God's love. But he gives it all the same. We are all as worthy as each other to receive it. As Timothy Radcliffe writes in his meditation, 'we need not fear to be naked. We are loved as we are.' Look at the story of the workers in the vineyard (Matthew 20.1-16). The vineyard owner doesn't discriminate between those who worked all day, and those who worked for only part of the day. All got what they were promised; all are equally important to God. As Kelly Connor reflects, it doesn't so much matter what has happened as how we respond to it. We have been given the power to forgive anyone anything, including ourselves. Peter Stanford points to the example of St Peter, who loved Jesus passionately and was closest to him, but kept getting it wrong:

> Peter said to Jesus, 'Master, it is wonderful for
> us to be here; so let us make three shelters,

> one for you, one for Moses and one for
> Elijah.' He did not know what he was saying.
> (Luke 9.33)

> 'Woman, I do not know him,' he said. Shortly
> afterwards someone else saw him and said,
> 'You are one of them too.' But Peter replied,
> 'I am not, my friend.' About an hour later
> another man insisted, saying, 'This fellow was
> certainly with him. Why, he is a Galilean.'
> Peter said, 'My friend, I do not know what
> you are talking about.' (Luke 22.57-60)

Despite these transgressions, Peter was forgiven and became the first Pope. None of us is perfect, but all of us are loved. As Paschal Uche highlights, we are made by love, to give and receive love. The theme running throughout this collection of meditations on the Stations of the Cross and Resurrection is overwhelmingly about love and about our relationships with each other and with God. Since the greatest commandment Christ gave us was to love one another as he loves us, this shouldn't be surprising. Maundy Thursday marks the beginning of the Easter Triduum, taking place immediately before the events reflected upon in this collection. 'Maundy' comes from the Latin word 'mandatum', which means 'commandment', and refers to the specific commandment Jesus gave to his disciples at the Last Supper: to love. Christ's life, his passion, death, and Resurrection, is quite literally an embodiment of God's love. But, as Chris Bain notes in the First Station, the love that is Jesus is not an easy kind of love. It is challenging. It can be uncomfortable, unacceptable, unrealistic and naïve. Mother Teresa famously said, 'I know God won't give me anything I can't handle. I just wish he didn't trust me so much.' As Anne Maguire's reflection testifies, God trusts in us, as we trust in him. He loves us. He is with us as we make our journey.

LIST OF CONTRIBUTORS

Chris Bain
Robin Baird-Smith
Ben Bano
Wendy Beckett
Ruth Burrows
Marie Collins
Kelly Connor
Rachel Denton
Joel Edwards
Paul Farmer
Anthony Feltham-White
Peter Hitchens
Sheila Hollins
Una Kroll
Bernard Longley
Anne Maguire
Danny McAllister
Margaret Mizen
Vincent Nichols
Timothy Radcliffe
Jonathan Romain
Lucy Russell
John Sentamu
Peter Stanford

Russell Stannard
Paschal Uche
Ann Widdecombe